W9-AGY-477

SandCastle™

Science Made Simple

You'll Cause a Stir When You Infer!

Esther Beck

Consulting Editors, Diane Craig, M.A./Reading Specialist
and Susan Kosel, M.A. Education

ABDO
Publishing Company

Published by ABDO Publishing Company, 4940 Viking Drive, Edina, Minnesota 55435.

Printed in the United States.

Credits
Edited by: Pam Price
Curriculum Coordinator: Nancy Tuminelly
Cover and Interior Design and Production: Mighty Media
Photo Credits: AbleStock, BananaStock Ltd., Creatas, Kelly Doudna, Photodisc, ShutterStock, Wewerka Photography

Library of Congress Cataloging-in-Publication Data

Beck, Esther.
    You'll cause a stir when you infer! / Esther Beck.
        p. cm. -- (Science made simple)
    ISBN 10 1-59928-626-2 (hardcover)
    ISBN 10 1-59928-627-0 (paperback)

    ISBN 13 978-1-59928-626-6 (hardcover)
    ISBN 13 978-1-59928-627-3 (paperback)
    1. Inference--Juvenile literature. 2. Reasoning--Juvenile literature. I. Title.

    BC199.I47B41 2006
    160--dc22
                                                                    2006023137

SandCastle Level: Transitional

SandCastle™ books are created by a professional team of educators, reading specialists, and content developers around five essential components—phonemic awareness, phonics, vocabulary, text comprehension, and fluency—to assist young readers as they develop reading skills and strategies and increase their general knowledge. All books are written, reviewed, and leveled for guided reading, early reading intervention, and Accelerated Reader® programs for use in shared, guided, and independent reading and writing activities to support a balanced approach to literacy instruction. The SandCastle™ series has four levels that correspond to early literacy development. The levels help teachers and parents select appropriate books for young readers.

Emerging Readers
(no flags)

Beginning Readers
(1 flag)

Transitional Readers
(2 flags)

Fluent Readers
(3 flags)

These levels are meant only as a guide. All levels are subject to change.

To **infer** is to decide something based on what you observe or already know.

Words used to talk about inferring:
conclude
guess
review
wonder

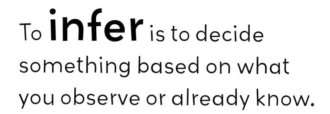

I found a fossil

of a .

I guess that this land was once covered by 🚰 .

The  is crying.

His mother gives him

a  and he stops.

I infer that the was hungry.

I play outside in the and get a sunburn.

I conclude that I should have used more SPF 45 .

You'll Cause a Stir When You Infer!

While Chad is
walking outside,
he spies a milkweed leaf
with a hole in its side.

I wonder
what would munch
on this leaf
for lunch?

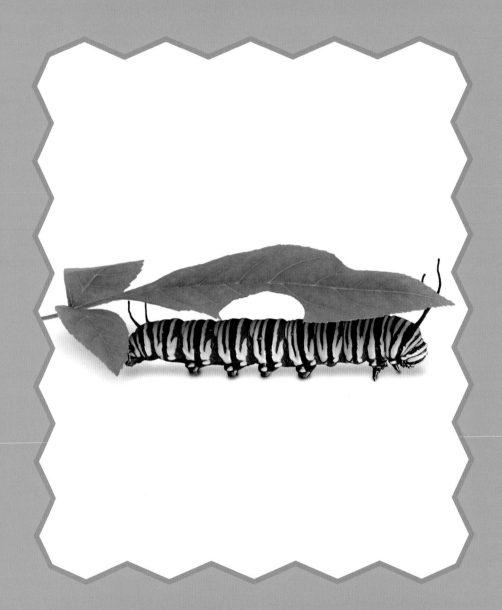

Looking closer, Chad sees a charming little fellow. "Why hello, Mr. Caterpillar, with stripes black, white, and yellow!"

See who I found when I looked around!

Chad reviews each clue and thinks it through. He guesses what creature played a role in chewing the hole.

I can infer that it was the caterpillar!

We Infer Every Day!

Mimi's potted flower is droopy.

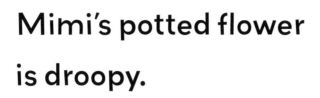

Mimi infers that it needs a drink of water.

Jackson drew on the sidewalk with chalk last night. This morning his art is gone.

Jackson concludes that it rained last night.

The players are cheering.

I guess that they just scored a goal.

The leaves are red and orange and have fallen to the ground.

What can you infer?

Glossary

conclusion – a judgment made after thinking carefully.

droopy – sagging or hanging down.

fossil – the remains or imprint of something that lived a long time ago.

guess – to give an answer based on what you think might be true.

milkweed – a plant that has purple flowers, milky sap, and large seed pods. Monarch caterpillars eat milkweed plants.

observe – to watch carefully.